Carolee's Cookbook for Kids—Salads

This Book Belongs To:

_____

Copyright ©2013 Janice Limb Myers

Published by LJM Publications, LLC

All rights reserved. No part of this publication may be reproduced or transmitted in any form or by any means, electronic or mechanical, including photocopying, recording, or any information storage and retrieval system, without the written permission of the copyright holder, except in the case of brief quotations embodied in critical reviews and certain other non-commercial uses permitted by copyright law.

Also by Janice Limb Myers:

Carolee Sings in the Christmas Choir, a Christmas Story for Children of All Ages

Link: http://bit.ly/caroleefans

Carolee Canta en el Coro Navideño, Una Relato Navideño para Niños de Todas las Edades

Link: http://bit.ly/caroleespanish

Table of Contents

Fruit Salads

Watermelon & Raspberries Salad	4
Apple, Grape & Celery Salad	6
Tropical Fruit Salad	8
Burst of Berries	10
Fruit Salad Pops	12

Veggie Salads

Carolee's Fav Chef Salad	14
Cobb Salad	16
Bean and Tomato Salad	18
Tomato and Mozzerella	20
Chopped Cabbage Supreme	22

Jello® Salads

Orange Go-Round	24

Meal Salads

Chicken Caesar	26
Quinoa, Spinach & Strawberry Salad	28
Broccoli and Pasta	30
Spinach and Bean	32

Carolee's Cookbook for Kids—Salads

Step 1: Gather Your Tools

- 1 paring knife
- Large spoon
- Large bowl
- Small bowl
- 4 Salad Plates
- Colander
- Measuring spoons
- Measuring cups
- Ice cream scoop

Step 2: Gather Ingredients

One watermelon, approximately 4 pounds
1 pint fresh raspberries
Juice of 1 lemon
1/4 cup sugar
Vanilla ice cream, for serving (optional)

Ask Carolee

Did you know that raspberries are amoung the world's most beloved fruits? They come from the same family as apples, apricots, blackberries, cherries, loquats, peaches, pears, plums, strawberries and almonds. In the U.S., raspberries are the third most popular berry behind strawberries (#1) and blueberries (#2).

There are over 200 species of raspberries. The most popular of them that are grown commercially and sold in the U.S. are classified into three groups: red raspberries, black raspberries and purple raspberries.

Watermelon & Raspberry Salad

Let's Make It!

STEP 1: Gather all your ingredients and tools together and set them on the counter or table where you plan to work.

STEP 2: Prepare the watermelon by cutting the rind off. Remove the seeds and cut the watermelon into 1-inch squares (cubes) to make about 4 cups of watermelon.

STEP 3: Gently place the watermelon cubes in a large bowl. Rinse the raspberries in the collander. Squeeze the juice from the lemon into a small dish, removing any seeds.

STEP 4: Gently add the raspberries, lemon juice, and sugar to the watermelon in the big bowl. Gently toss with a large spoon to combine. Let stand on the counter at least 30 minutes, tossing once in a while, until all the sugar is dissolved.

STEP 5: Once the sugar is all dissolved in the juice, cover the container with a lid or plastic wrap. Place it in the refrigerator to chill.

STEP 6:: Just before serving, place a scoop of vanilla ice cream in a dish. Add a large spoon full of watermelon-raspberry salad on top. Serve immediately.

OPTIONS: This sald is great served by itself without the ice cream. Tear a lettuce leaf for each serving. Place it on the plate and top with a large spoonful of the watermelon-raspberry mixture. Serve as a side dish with dinner.

Makes 6-8 Servings

Carolee's Cookbook for Kids—Salads

Step 2: Gather Ingredients

1/4 cup chopped pecans
2 celery stalks
1 Granny Smith apple
1 cup seedless red grapes
1 tablespoon white-wine vinegar
1 tablespoon extra-virgin olive oil
Celery leaves

Step 1: Gather Your Tools

- Paring knife
- Cutting board
- Apple corer
- 4 small bowls
- Baking sheet
- 2 Oven its
- Large serving bowl

Ask Carolee

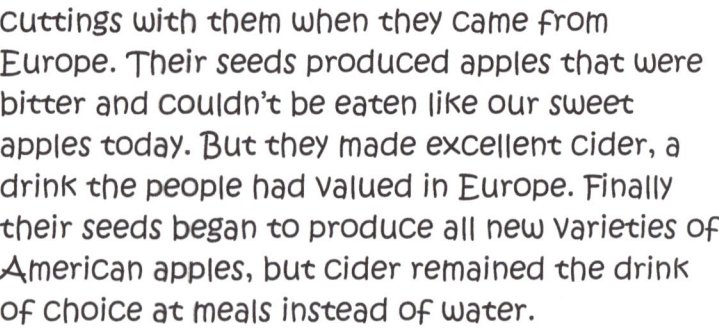

Did you know that apple harvesting began in the U.S. by settlers at Jamestown in 1607. They brought seeds and cuttings with them when they came from Europe. Their seeds produced apples that were bitter and couldn't be eaten like our sweet apples today. But they made excellent cider, a drink the people had valued in Europe. Finally their seeds began to produce all new varieties of American apples, but cider remained the drink of choice at meals instead of water.

Apple, Grape & Celery Salad

Let's Make It!

STEP 1: Gather all your ingredients and tools together and set them on the counter or table where you plan to work.

STEP 2: Preheat oven to 350 degrees.

STEP 3: Prepare your ingredients as follows:

- Carefully chop the pecans to medium size pieces using a knife and cutting board. Place into a small dish. Set aside.

- Clean the celery stalks, cutting of the ends. Then carefully chop the celery stalks into very thin slices, cutting on the diagonal. Place in a bowl and set aside.

- Core the apple with an apple corer. Cut the pieces into thin slices into a small dish. Set aside. (See photo.)

- Wash the red grapes and slice them into halves into a small dish. Set aside.

STEP 4: Spread the chopped pecans on a baking sheet, and bake until lightly browned, only 4 to 6 minutes. Remove to cool.

STEP 5: In a large bowl, combine the celery, apples, grapes. Mix the vinegar and oil in a small bowl. Use a spoon to drizzle the oil mixture over the fruit in bowl. Toss together gently to combine.

STEP 6 : Garnish with celery leaves.

Makes 2 Serving

Carolee's Cookbook for Kids—Salads

Step 2: Gather Ingredients

1 pineapple, cut into chunks
1 pound strawberries, quartered
Zest from 1 lime, plus 2 tablespoons juice
1/2 cup fresh mint leaves
1/4 cup coconut (chips or shredded)

Ask Carolee

Did you know you can clean strawberries with a straw? There's no prep work except to wash your strawberries. Then just take a strawberry in one hand, and a straw in the other. Put the straw at the bottom of the strawberry and push firmly. It will go through the strawberry and out the top, pushing out the core and top leaves of the strawberry. The core will remain in the straw, so periodically you'll need to squeeze the cores out of the straw to make room for more.

You'll have perfectly cored strawberries and less waste than using a knife. Then slice, quarter or whatever you choose to do to use the strawberries in this and other recipes.

Step 1: Gather Your Tools

- Large bowl
- Large spoon
- Knife
- Large bowl
- Zester
- Measuring spoons

Tropical Fruit Salad

Let's Make It!

STEP 1

Gather all your ingredients and tools together and set them on the counter or table where you plan to work.

STEP 2

Using a sharp knife and cutting board, cut both ends off the pineapple. Stand it up on end and work your way around the pineapple, peeling off the exterior of the pineapple down to the pine. Onxce the exterior is removed, slice the pineapple in 3/4" to 1" slices, then cut those into chunks. Place chunks in a large bowl.

STEP 3

Next let's clean the strawberries. Rinse the strawberries in water and lightly dry with a paper towel. Remove the leaves and core with a knife or use Carolee's tip to do it with a straw (see Did You Know?). Slice each strawberry in half and then in half again to create quarters. Add to the pineapple in the bowl.

STEP 4

Next, use a zester or small food grater to zest the sides of one lime. For a description on how to do this, see the "Did You Know" section.

Then cut the lime in half and squeeze juice into a small bowl. For 2 tablespoons of juice you will need two limes. Measure 2 tablespoons of juice and add to the fruit in the bowl. Stir.

STEP 5

Sprinkle with coconut and decorate with mint leaves. Serve immediately or cover and refrigerate until ready to serve.

Makes 6 Servings

Carolee's Cookbook for Kids—Salads

Step 2: Gather Ingredients

3 tablespoons light-brown sugar
2 tablespoons freshly squeezed lime juice
3 purple or red plums (12-16 oz)
2 cups seedless red grapes
1 pint blackberries
1/2 pint blueberries

Ask Carolee

How should we take care of a wooden cutting board? After each use, wash wooden boards with a bit of soap, rinse in hot water, wipe clean, and allow to dry upright.

To maintain your board, every few weeks generously sprinkle coarse salt over the surface of the board, rub it with a sliced lemon, then rinse well with hot water. If your cutting boards are made from butcher block, once a month apply a small amount of *mineral oil* or *beeswax*, rubbing it with a lint-free cloth in the direction of the wood grain. Wipe off excess oil and dry board overnight. Warning: Do *not* use olive oil or vegetable oil as they will go rancid on your board.

Step 1: Gather Your Tools

- Mixing spoon
- Measuring spoons
- Measuring cups
- Paring knife
- Cutting Board
- Large bowl
- Small bowl

Burst of Berries Salad

Let's Make It!

STEP 1

Gather all your ingredients and tools together and set them on the counter or table where you plan to work.

STEP 2:

Roll the limes around on a hard work surface using a little pressure from the palm of your hand. This helps to release the juices. Then cut them in half and squeeze the juice into a small bowl. Using a measuring spoon, measure 2 tablespoons of lime juice and place it in a large bowl.

Add the brown sugar to the lime juice in the large bowl, and stir together well. Let stand 10 minutes to allow the sugar to dissolve.

STEP 3

While you're waiting for the lime juice mixture, you can begin work on your fruit. First, wash the fruit before using. Then remove the pits from the plums and cut them into 1/2-inch pieces. Check to be sure the sugar has dissolved in the lime juice by stirring it again. Then add the plums to the bowl.

STEP 4

Next add the grapes, blackberries and blueberries and gently toss to combine with the lime juice.

STEP 5

Cover the dish with plastic wrap and set in refrigerator until ready to serve. This salad can be refrigerated for up to 24 hours.

OPTION: Before serving, add a few fresh mint leaves.

Makes 2 Serving

Carolee's Cookbook for Kids—Salads

Step 2: Gather Ingredients

1 peach

2 kiwis

3 ounces blueberries

4 ounces strawberries

1 1/2 to 2 cups 100 percent white grape juice

Step 1: Gather Your Tools

- Eight 3-oz popsicle molds
- Popsicle sticks
- Paring knife
- Cutting board
- Four small bowls

Ask Carolee

Did you know that the popsicle was invented in 1905 by an 11-year-old boy named Frank Epperson? He left his fruit-flavored drink outside on the porch with a stir-stick in it. The drink froze to the stick and Frank thought it tasted good. It was 18 more years before he applied for a patent for Epsicle ice pop, which his children re-named the Popsicle. The patent is now owned by the Good Humor Company.

Fruit Salad Pops

Let's Make It!

This is one of the easiest and most fun ways we've learned to make a Fruit Salad! They're a healthy treat for parties or any day of the year.

STEP 1
Gather all your ingredients and tools together and set them on the counter or table where you plan to work.

STEP 2
First, wash all the fruit.

Then peel the peach with a vegetable peeler and cut it in 1/2-inch slices and place in small dish.

Peel the 2 kiwis and slice them into 1/4" rounds and place in a small bowl.

Pour the blueberries in a small bowl.

Hull the strawberries. (See Ask Carolee in the Tropical Fruit Salad recipe to learn to hull strawberries with a straw.) Then cut the strawberries in halves and place in a small bowl.

STEP 3
Now for some fun! Arrange the fruit in the ice pop molds, being sure the pieces fit snugly. Following the picture at the left will help. Do you see how the kiwi slices fit nicely at the top of the mold?

Once the molds are filled with fruit, carefully pour enough white grape juice into each mold to just cover the fruit and fill the mold.

Insert popsicle sticks and freeze until they are solid, about 4 to 6 hours. Popsicles will remain fresh in the freezer for up to three weeks, but they won't last that long!

Makes 8 Servings

Carolee's Cookbook for Kids—Salads

Step 2: Gather Ingredients

1/3 cup low-fat buttermilk
1/3 cup reduced-fat sour cream
2 tablespoons cider vinegar
1 tablespoon honey
1 large head Boston lettuce
1 pound sliced roasted turkey breast
1 avocado
1 small red onion
4 carrots, cut into matchstick pieces
1 cup alfalfa sprouts
4 ounces Monterey Jack cheese

Step 1: Gather Your Tools

- Small wire whisk
- Small spoon
- Small bowl
- 4 Salad Plates
- 1 paring knife

Ask Carolee

Did you know the chef's Salad has been around for nearly 100 years? It is estimated today that 30% of food in the U.S. gets thrown away. When you're the chef, you can put whatever you want in your Chef's Salad, including some leftovers. Typically, it always includes meat such as ham, chicken or turkey, cheese, and some salad vegetables on top of a bed of lettuce and is served as a full meal salad.

Carolee's Fav Chef's Salad

Let's Make It!

STEP 1: Gather all your ingredients and tools together and set them on the counter or table where you plan to work.

STEP 2: Measure the following ingredients and place them all in the small bowl:

- Buttermilk
- Sour Cream
- Vinegar
- Honey

Using the wire whisk or a spoon, stir thoroughly. Set the bowl of dressing aside.

STEP 3: Tear the lettuce into pieces and divide it among the four serving plates.

STEP 4: Prepare the ingredients. Cut the turkey and cheese into strips. Peel, pit and slice the avocado. Slice the onion. Peel the carrots and cut into small strips called matchsticks (because they look like wooden matches). Loosen the spouts so they're fluffy.

STEP 5: Evenly divide the following ingredients between the four bowls of lettuce:

- Turkey
- Avocado
- Onion
- Carrots
- Sprouts
- Cheese

Makes 4 Servings

Carolee likes to arrange these ingredients to make a pretty and colorful salad. See how pretty you can make yours!

STEP 6: Using a spoon, drizzle the dressing over the top of the salad. Serve along with the remaining dressing.

OPTIONS: Try using chicken or ham along with different vegetables for variety. Raisins or cranberries go well with this salad, too, and add a touch of sweetness.

Carolee's Cookbook for Kids—Salads

Step 2: Gather Ingredients

3 slices bacon
1 cup low-fat or regular buttermilk
1/4 cup light or regular mayonnaise
1 tablespoon red-wine vinegar
1/2 cup crumbled blue or feta cheese
2 heads Boston lettuce (1 pound total)
6 ounces deli turkey
4 plum tomatoes
4 large hard-cooked eggs
1 avocado

Step 1: Gather Your Tools

- Small wire whisk
- Medium bowl
- Large bowl
- Medium skillet
- Paper towels
- Paring knife

Ask Carolee

There's a legend about how the Cobb Salad was created. It goes like this: Late one night in 1937, the owner of The Brown Derby in in Hollywood was hungry and was looking around the kitchen for a snack. When he opened the refrigerator, he pulled out a bunch of stuff: lettuce, an avocado, some romaine, watercress, tomatoes, some cold breast of chicken, a hard-boiled egg, chives, cheese and some crisp bacon. The Cobb Salad was then added to their regular menu.

Carolee's Cobb Salad

Let's Make It!

STEP 1

In a medium bowl, whisk together the buttermilk, mayonnaise, and vinegar. Gently fold in the cheese. Carefully season with salt (not too much) and set the dressing aside.

STEP 2

In a medium skillet, cook the bacon on medium heat, turning occasionally, until crisp, 5 to 8 minutes. Transfer the bacon to a paper-towel-lined plate, and allow to drain. When it's cool, break the bacon into bite-size pieces.

STEP 3

Cut the turkey into bite-sized pieces. Chop the tomatoes. Slice the hard-cooked eggs. Peel and slice the avocado.

STEP 4

Tear the lettuce into bite-sized pieces and put it in a large bowl. Decorate the top of the salad with the bacon, turkey, tomatoes, eggs, and avocado. Serve salad with dressing alongside it for a full meal.

OPTIONS: Add carrot matchstick pieces, tomatoes, cucumbers and other salad vegetables that are your favorites.

Makes 4 Servings

Carolee's Cookbook for Kids—Salads

Step 2: Gather Ingredients

1 14 oz. can cannellini beans (or other white beans)

1 pint grape tomatoes, halved

4 scallions, thinly sliced

2 tablespoons olive oil

1 tablespoon fresh lemon juice

Ask Carolee

Most nutritionists believe that we eat too much red meat. But reducing our meat consumption requires that we replace the protein in our meals. Beans are one of the best ways to do that.

Beans are high in dietary fiber, low in fats and usually contain no cholesterol. In addition beans are much more versatile, there are far more varieties to choose from than meat, and they're much less expensive as meat.

Step 1: Gather Your Tools

- Can opener
- Paring knife
- Medium bowl
- Paring knife
- Cutting board
- Small bowl
- Measuring spoons

Bean and Tomato Salad

Let's Make It!

STEP 1

Gather all your ingredients and tools together and set them on the counter or table where you plan to work.

STEP 2

Let's prepare the ingredients.

- First, open the can of cannellini beans and rinse them with cold water in a colander. Drain completely and place in medium bowl.

- Rinse the grape tomatoes and cut them carefully into halves on a cutting board. Add to the beans in the bowl.

- Thinly slice the scallions on the cutting board. Then add them to the bowl.

- Roll the lemon around on your work surface placing a little weight with the palm of your hand. Then place the lemon on the cutting board and cut it in half and squeeze the juice into a small bowl. Measure out 1 tablespoon of juice and add to the bowl with the beans.

STEP 3

Measure the oil and add it to the bowl. Toss all the ingredients together. Season with a pinch of salt and pepper.

STEP 4

Serve immediately or cover and store in the refrigerator for up to 24 hours. Storing for an hour or so will allow the flavors to mingle better before serving.

Makes 4 Servings

Carolee's Cookbook for Kids—Salads

Step 2: Gather Ingredients

1/2 cup packed fresh basil leaves
2 tablespoons olive oil
2 tablespoons white-wine vinegar
3 ounces fresh goat cheese or mozarella
3 medium tomatoes
Salt and pepper

Step 1: Gather Your Tools

- Measuring cups
- Measuring spoons
- Small wire whisk
- Blender
- Dental floss
- Paring knife
- Serving platter
- Spoon

Ask Carolee

Three of the most common examples of vinegar are cider, balsamic, and white vinegars. Cider vinegar is typically made from apples, and is created by crushing apples in a press to make juice, which is fermented into cider.

Balsamic vinegar is a product of Italy, primarily from Modena, made with white Trebbiano grapes which are pressed and aged in barrels and is sweet enough to even be used in desserts.

White vinegar is made by oxidizing distilled grain alcohol. It tends to be the most sour and is often used as a clean fluid.

Tomato and Mozzarella Salad

Let's Make It!

STEP 1

Gather all your ingredients and tools together and set them on the counter or table where you plan to work.

STEP 2

Note: Set aside a few of the basil leaves for garnishing the salad.

Measure the fresh basil leaves and pour into a blender. Measure and add the olive oil, vinegar, and 1 tablespoon of water to the blender.

STEP 3

Process in the blender until smooth, 2 to 3 minutes. Season the mixture with a dash of salt and pepper and set aside. This is your salad dressing, called a vinaigrette.

STEP 4

With dental floss or a warm knife, slice the cheese into thin slices. If you use a warm knife, wipe it clean after each slice so it will run smoothly through the cheese on the next cut.

With a sharp knife, remove the core from the tomatoes and slice them crosswise into about 1/2-inch thick slices.

STEP 5

Arrange the tomatoes on a serving plate and top them with the cheese. Use a spoon to drizzle lightly with the dressing. Serve the remainder of the dressing with the salad for individual servings.

Garnish your salad with a few saved basil leaves to make your salad pleasing to the eye. Serve.

Makes 4 Servings

Carolee's Cookbook for Kids—Salads

Step 2: Gather Ingredients

3 ounces light oil
3 ounces vinegar
1/3 to 2/3 cups sugar
1/4 cup water
2 pounds cabbage
2 carrots
1/2 green pepper
Green onions

Step 1: Gather Your Tools

- Food grater
- Vegetable peeler
- Cutting board
- Knife
- Measuring cups (with ounce measure)
- Measuring spoons
- Large bowl
- Medium jar or container with lid
- Spoon

Ask Carolee

Measurements all Chefs should know:

1 tablespoon (tbsp) =	3 teaspoons (tsp)
1/4 cup =	4 tablespoons
1/2 cup =	8 tablespoons
1 cup =	16 tablespoons
1 pint (pt) =	2 cups
1 quart (qt) =	2 pints
4 cups =	1 quart
1 gallon (gal) =	4 quarts

Chopped Cabbage Salad

Let's Make It!

STEP 1: Gather all your ingredients and tools together and set them on the counter or table where you plan to work.

STEP 2: Measure the following ingredients and place them all in a jar or medium dish with a lid:
- Oil
- Vinegar
- Sugar
- Water

Makes 6 Servings

Tighten the lid, then shake well for one full minute. This will dissolve the sugar in the liquids.

STEP 3: Next you will grate the vegetables for your salad. This can be done in a variety of ways depending on the grating tools you have available in your kitchen. You can ask an adult what they think will be the best tool. I use an electric Pro Salad Shooter as it makes quick work of the job. You may have a food processor that will work or a hand grater.

Shred the cabbage into a large bowl. Then peel and shred the carrots. Add to cabbage in bowl.

Using a cutting board and knife, chop the top and bottom off the green pepper and remove the seeds and tissue from inside. Then cut it in half and chop it into small pieces. Add the green pepper to the cabbage in the bowl.

If you are using green onions, cut two into small pieces using the green portion if desired. Add to the bowl.

STEP 4: Shake the jar or container with the dressing again briefly to remix the ingredients. Then pour the mixture over the cabbage and stir with a large spoon.

Cover and refrigerate. This salad will keep for a week in the refrigerator. The longer it marinates, the better the taste.

Carolee's Cookbook for Kids—Salads

Step 1: Gather Your Tools

- Large bowl
- Medium sauce pan
- Measuring cup
- 6-Cup gelatin
- Cutting Board
- Paring knife
- Straw for cleaning strawberries (optional)
- Canned cooking spray

Step 2: Gather Ingredients

1-1/2 cups boiling water
1 pkg. (0.6 oz.) Orange Flavored JELL-O®
2 cups cold club soda
1 can (11 oz.) mandarin oranges, drained
1 cup sliced fresh strawberries

Ask Carolee

You can speed up the setting process of Jello®. Follow the directions on the box to add boiling water to the gelatin mix. Stir very well to dissolve the mix in the hot water. Then in the next step, add the required amount of water in ice cubes instead of water. Stir until the ice dissolves. Continue with the recipe.

To use this method with this recipe you would have to make ice cubes from 2 cups of club soda (the second liquid).

Orange-Strawberry Go-Round

Let's Make It!

STEP 1: Gather all your ingredients and tools together and set them on the counter or table where you plan to work.

STEP 2: In a medium sized sauce pan pour 1 1/2 cups of water. Turn heat to medium.

STEP 3: Meanwhile, pour the orange-flavored Jello® mix into a large bowl. When the water comes to a boil, add the boiling water to the gelatin mix. Stir for 2 minutes until the gelatin is completely dissolved.

STEP 4: Measure and stir in the cold club soda. This gives the salad the sparkle and shimmer. Refrigerate 1-1/2 hours or until thickened in the bowl.

STEP 5: Prepare the fruit by draining the juice from the can of mandarin oranges. Discard the juice. After the Jello® has thickened in the refrigerator, add the oranges to the gelatin mix.

Wash the strawberries and remove the cores as shown in "Did You Know" for Tropical Fruit Salad. Slice the strawberries. Add them to the gelatin mix.

STEP 6: Stir the fruit and gelatin. Spray a 6-cup gelatin mold with cooking spray and pour the mixture into it.

STEP 7: Refrigerate for 4 hours or until firm. To unmold, fill the sink about half full with warm water. Hold the mold in the warm water carefully so the water doesn't go over the edges and into the mold. Jiggle the mold slightly and when you see some movement, remove the mold from the water. Turn it upside down on a serving platter. Let sit for a few seconds, then lift the mold off the salad. Serve immediately or refrigerate until serving.

Makes 6 Servings

Carolee's Cookbook for Kids—Salads

Step 2: Gather Ingredients

1 1/2 cups low-fat buttermilk
2 tablespoons fresh lemon juice
1 garlic clove
1/4 cup grated Parmesan cheese
3 boneless, skinless chicken breast halves
2 thick slices multigrain bread
1 tablespoon olive oil
1/4 cup mayonnaise (light or regular)
2 medium heads romaine lettuce

Ask Carolee

1. Sometimes you may not have buttermilk in the refrigerator. You can make it by adding one tablespoon of vinegar to one cup of milk. Stir it and measure out the quantity you need for your recipe.

2. When squeezing lemons, first lay the lemon on its side and roll it back and forth under the palm of your hand for about 30 seconds, pushing down a little bit. It will loosen up the juice and make it easier to get a good amount of juice from the lemon.

3. What's a "pinch" of something? It's about 1/8 teaspoon, but usually the smallest measuring spoon is 1/4 teaspoon, so cooks like me just take a pinch of the spice between our thumb and forefinger. That's about 1/8 teaspoon.

Step 1: Gather Your Tools

- Garlic press
- Paring knife
- Baking sheet
- Measuring spoons
- Measuring cups
- 2 small bowls
- Medium mixing bowl
- Re-sealable plastic bag
- Pastry brush
- 2 Oven mitts
- Large serving bowl, salad tongs or serving pieces

Chicken Caesar Salad

Let's Make It!

STEP 1: Gather all your ingredients and tools together and set them on the counter or table where you plan to work.

STEP 2: Heat the broiler and place a rack 4 inches from the heat. Line a rimmed baking sheet with aluminum foil.

STEP 3: Peel the clove of garlic and place it inside the garlic press. Squeeze as hard as you can so the garlic comes through the tool. You may have to use a knife to get it to fall off the backside of the press.

Put it in a medium bowl. Squeeze the juice out of the lemons into a small dish. Measure the lemon juice and add it to the garlic along with the buttermilk, and Parmesan cheese. Stir with a wire wisk. Add a pinch of salt and pepper.

STEP 4: Place chicken in a re-sealable plastic bag. Measure out 1/2 cup of the dressing and set it aside for the salad. Then add the remainder from the bowl to the chicken in the bag. Refrigerate the chicken at least 30 minutes and up to 24 hours with the dressing on it.

STEP 5: Meanwhile, you can make the croutons. First lightly brush on some oil on a baking sheet Brush both sides of the bread with oil. Broil until toasted, 1 to 2 minutes per side. Cut into 1-inch pieces and set aside, reserving the baking sheet for the next step.

STEP 6: After the chicken has marinated, remove it from the refrigerator and put it on the same baking sheet. Empty the remaining marinade down the drain and close the bag tightly so it won't make a mess. Place the chicken under the broiler and broil until it is cooked throughout, 10 to 16 minutes. Remove the pan from the oven with oven mitts to protect your hands.

STEP 7: Let the chicken rest 5 minutes. Then thinly slice it crosswise.

In a large bowl, stir together the mayonnaise and the buttermilk mixture you saved. Tear the romaine into bite-size pieces. Add the romaine lettuce, chicken, and croutons; toss to combine. Serve immediately.

Makes 6 Servings

Carolee's Cookbook for Kids—Salads

Step 2: Gather Ingredients

1/2 cup red-wine vinegar
1/3 cup olive oil
2 pounds fresh sliced mushrooms
1 1/2 cups quinoa
1 pound baby spinach
1 pint fresh strawberries
1/2 red onion, sliced (optional)
8 ounces feta cheese, crumbled

Ask Carolee

Quinoa (pronounced KEEN-wah) has been a stable food in South and Central America for thousands of years. The tiny seeds of this plant were highly regarded by the Incas. The Incas referred to quinoa as *chisaya mama*, or "mother of all grains." But in reality, quinoa is actually an herb, not a grain, that thrives in cold, high elevations like the Andes Mountains. While it's mostly grown in South America, farmers in the Rocky Mountains and in the Pacific Northwest have recently begun cultivating quinoa as well. It is agreed that quinoa is a healthy food and add a spark to this salad.

Step 1: Gather Your Tools

- Small wire whisk
- Small bowl and medium bowl
- Measuring spoons
- Measuring cups
- Paring Knife
- Large baking sheet
- Spatula
- Medium saucepan with lid
- Large serving bowl
- Serving tongs

Quinoa, Spinach, and Strawberry Salad

Let's Make It!

STEP 1: Gather all your ingredients and tools together and set them on the counter or table where you plan to work.

STEP 2: Set a broiler rack about 4 inches from the broiler heat source and turn heat on to the broil setting. In a small bowl, use a whisk to stir vinegar, oil, 1 teaspoon salt, and 1/4 teaspoon pepper. Wash and drain the spinach so it will be dry when you need it.

STEP 3: Clean mushrooms and remove stems. Cut the caps in half. On a large rimmed baking sheet, toss the mushrooms with half the dressing you made in Step 1 and save the rest for later.

STEP 4: Broil the mushrooms, tossing occasionally with a spatula until most of the liquid has evaporated and mushrooms are tender, 10 to 12 minutes for regular mushrooms, about 20-25 minutes for Shitake mushrooms.

STEP 5: Meanwhile, in a medium saucepan, combine the quinoa, 3 cups water, and 1 1/2 teaspoons salt. Bring to a boil; reduce heat to medium/low. Cover the pan, and simmer until liquid has been absorbed, about 15 to 20 minutes.

STEP 6: Wash strawberries. Dry. Remove stems and leaves. Slice into a medium-sized bowl.

STEP 7: Place dry spinach in a large bowl; add hot mushrooms, quinoa, strawberries, sliced red onion (if your family likes it) and reserved dressing. Toss to combine (spinach will wilt slightly from the heat). Top with crumbled feta cheese, and serve immediately.

If you can't serve it immediately, then wait till just before serving to toss the spinach, cooled mushrooms, onion, cooled quinoa and strawberries with the reserved dressing and top with crumbled feta cheese. This will mean the spinach won't wilt in the salad.

Makes 6 Servings

Carolee's Cookbook for Kids—Salads

Step 1: Gather Your Tools

- Large pot
- Colander
- Paring knife
- Vegetable peeler
- Measuring spoons
- Measuring cup
- Large skillet with cover
- Large bowl
- Large spoon

Step 2: Gather Ingredients

1/2 pound plain or whole-wheat fusilli
2 pounds fresh broccoli
3 tablespoons vegetable oil
1/2 teaspoon red-pepper flakes (opt)
1/4 cup rice vinegar
2 tablespoons smooth peanut butter
3 tablespoons soy sauce
1/2 bunch scallions

Ask Carolee

"*Fusilli*" are long, thick, corkscrew shaped pasta. It is traditionally "spun" by pressing and rolling a small rod over the thin strips of pasta to wind them around it in a corkscrew shape. Then it is allowed to dry in that shape.

"*Al dente*" describes pasta, rice or beans that have been cooked so they are still firm but not hard. You can test your pasta during cooking to be sure it's not overcooked.

Broccoli & Pasta Salad

Let's Make It!

STEP 1: Gather all your ingredients and tools together and set them on the counter or table where you plan to work.

STEP 2: In a large pot of boiling salted water, cook pasta until al dente according to package instructions (see Did You Know). Drain, and rinse under cold water in a colander. Set aside.

STEP 3: While the water is coming to a boil, trim 1 inch from the stem end of broccoli stalks. Using a vegetable peeler or paring knife, peel outer layer of stalks. Separate the florets into bite-sized pieces. Many will just break off, but you may need a knife to separate some of them.

STEP 4: Clean the scallions cutting on the end and removing the outside membrane. Then carefully slice them crosswise to get 1/2 cup.

Carefully heat 1 tablespoon of oil in a large skillet over medium heat. Add the pepper flakes, broccoli florets, and 3/4 cup water. Cover and cook until broccoli is al dente (crisp-tender) about 6 to 8 minutes. Uncover and cook until the liquid has evaporated and broccoli is tender, about 2 to 4 minutes.

STEP 5: In a large bowl, add the remainder of the oil (2 tablespoons oil), the vinegar, peanut butter, and soy sauce and whisk until smooth. Add cooled pasta, broccoli, and scallions. Toss with a spoon to combine. Serve immediately, or cover and refrigerate and serve chilled.

Makes 6 Servings

Carolee's Cookbook for Kids—Salads

Step 2: Gather Ingredients

3 tablespoons olive oil
1 tablespoon finely sliced lemon zest, plus 2 tablespoons fresh lemon juice
1/2 teaspoon Dijon mustard
3 cups cooked pinto beans (drained) or 2 cans of pinto beans
8 ounces fresh spinach (4 cups)
1/2 cup parsley
2 scallions

Step 1: Gather Your Tools

- Cutting board
- Paring knife
- Wire whisk
- Zester
- Medium bowl
- Colander
- Medium pot with lid

Ask Carolee

Let's talk about zesting lemons or other fruit. The peel of a citrus fruit such as lemons, oranges, contains two top layers.

The zest is the outermost part of the rind. On a lemon, zest is the yellow part of the peel on the outside of a lemon. The zest is shiny, brightly colored, and textured; it is the outer surface of the fruit that you can see. The pitch is the inner white part of the peel and is bitter, so you only want to use the colored part of the fruit for zesting.

Spinach and Bean Salad

Let's Make It!

STEP 1: Gather all your ingredients and tools together and set them on the counter where you plan to work.

STEP 2: Let's do all the chopping first. Using your cutting board and a sharp knife, carefully chop the parsley and thinly slide the scallions. Set them aside to use in Step 5.

STEP 3: (Read Carolee's note to the left about zesting.) To make the lemon zest, first wash and dry the lemons. You'll probably need 2 lemons to get enough juice. Using a small zester or grater, scrape the sides of the lemon on the zester to grate off only the yellow part of the lemon (the zest) until you get enough to fill a tablespoon.

STEP 4: In a medium bowl, whisk together the oil, lemon juice, and mustard. Then stir in the drained beans. (If you are using canned pinto beans, drain the beans in a colander and rinse them with cold water.)

STEP 5: Add 1 inch of water to a medium pot. Add a pinch of salt and bring to a boil on the stove top.

Add the spinach to the boiling water and cover the pot. Cook until the spinach is limp and wilted, 2 to 4 minutes. Drain the spinach in a colander until all the moisture is gone. Then pour the drained spinach into the bowl with the beans. Add the parsley, scallions, and lemon zest. Then toss to combine. Serve or cover and refrigerate until serving.

Makes 6-8 Servings

Best Selling Carolee Book!

Introducing Carolee's #1 Best Selling Book

This Year's Sure-to-Be Christmas Classic

Carolee joins the children's Christmas Choir, planning a very special performance on Christmas Eve, when Carolee hopes to become a singing Superstar. Oh, did I tell you Carolee is an angel? And she's only 8 years old!

Miss Marie, the choir director, is busy trying to get everything ready for the performance at which a very special guest will be in the audience. But a few short days before the performance, something goes terribly wrong at choir practice.

Will Carolee become the Superstar she hopes to be . . . or something else entirely? What role will the special guest play in the outcome? You'll never guess how things end up for Miss Marie, the choir, and Carolee!

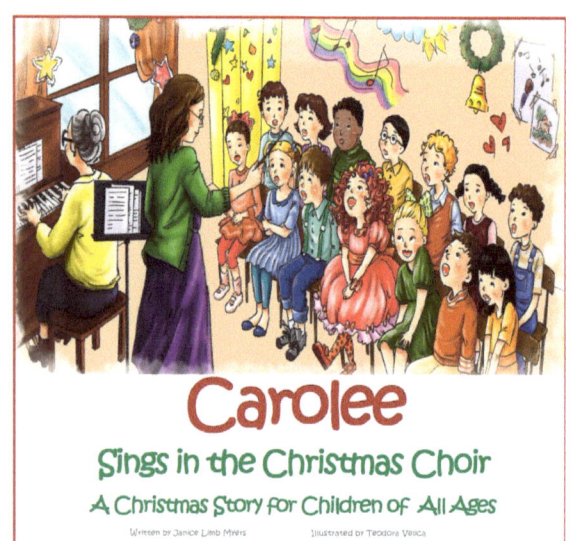

Paperback and Kindle

http://bit.ly/Carolee2

Over 35,000 sold!

Watch the Trailer:
http://bit.ly/CaroleeTrailer

Also in Spanish!

Carolee Canta en el Coro Navideño - Una Relato Navideño para Niños de Todas las Edades

Carolee es parte de un coro celestial – porque ella es un ángel - y este coro está planeando hacer una actuación muy especial en Noche Buena, donde Carolee espera convertirse en una verdadera Super Estrella del canto. Pero unos días antes de la actuación, la Señorita Marie, la directora del coro, está ocupada tratando de poner todo en orden y sabe que algo está faltando.

¿Cuándo las cosas van mal en los ensayos del coro, Carolee podrá convertirse en la Super Estrella que espera ser... o en alguien totalmente diferente? Nunca adivinarás cómo terminan las cosas para la Señorita Marie y para Carolee.

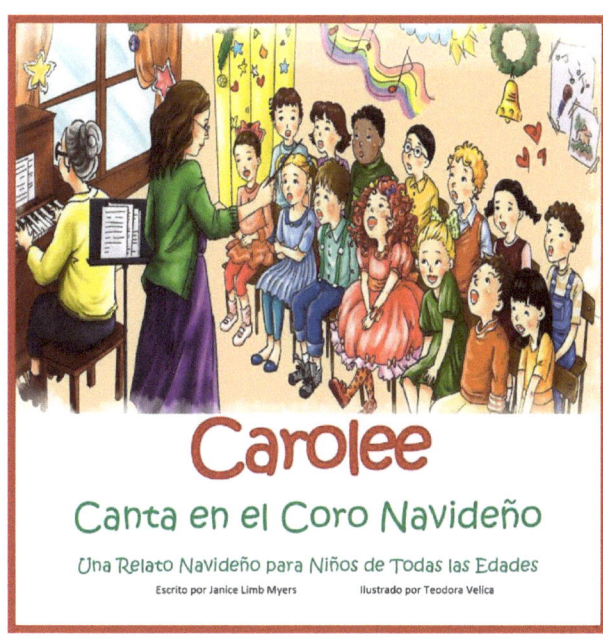

libro de bolsillo y Kindle

http://bit.ly/CaroleeSpanish

!más de 35.000 vendidos!

Watch the Trailer:
http://bit.ly/ CaroleeSpanishTrailer

Get a FREE Carolee Coloring Book!

Get Your Free
Carolee Coloring Book and Fun Activities

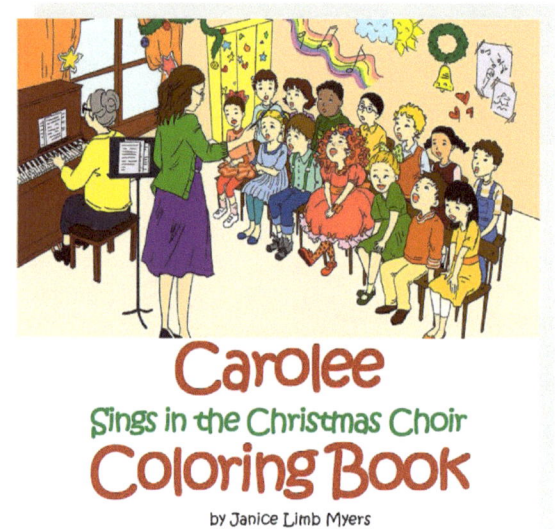

www.Carolee.org
Register Now

and your coloring book will be on its way to you!

And One Last Thing . . .

Thank you!

Carolee and I want to thank you for purchasing Carolee's first cookbook for kids. If you enjoyed reading and using this book, I'd be very grateful if you would post a short review on Amazon. I read all the reviews personally and each review really makes a difference.

Please click on the review link on this book's page on Amazon.com where you purchased the book.

Thanks again for your support and we hope your family enjoys Carolee's recipes